NOW THEY ARE

People say, "Babies aren't
born with a book"

MeChele Kelly-Haire

outskirts
press

Diploma

Remember to have the doctor sign your diploma.

This book is dedicated to
My Dearest Children
Toshio Bernard,
Tyler Brandon, and T'ne Breez

Contents

When a woman first finds out that she is pregnant, it was either planned with her husband, boyfriend, partner, or without. Truth is ladies, we are truly in control of when this happens. Why, because we truly rule the world; therefore, be very mindful of the choices you make, and who you choose to make them with. As you embark on this journey, remember it will be your most courageous journey of a lifetime. Therefore remember, birth control prevents pregnancy 99% of the time, and condoms prevent STD's. So practice safe sex unless you want a gift you can't literally give back. E-V-E-R. *NEWS FLASH: When a female finds out that she is pregnant, she gain 5-7 years and become a parent instantly. When a male finds out that he is about to become a parent, before he can take it all in, he needs to rush out and finish being a boy before he can jump into the whole parent/sacrifice mode. Males instantly feel like their loosing themselves, while females instantly understand they're sharing themselves. So understand ladies, they are nowhere near where we want them to be, nor where we are mentally. Be patient.* More importantly understand this: When you conceive a child, you don't know what genes were transported in order to create this child. Good genes, bad genes, third generational genes, first generational genes, mom's genes, daddy genes, or any other ancestor's genes dangling out there. You don't know who you're getting, just like the child doesn't know who they ended up with. Therefore, work hard to change the world to be a better place. In the meantime, try not to deprive them from what society says to be a "normal" childhood; therefore, they won't deprive you from what society says is "normal" parenthood. The best part of it all, it will be the most loving, fulfilling, challenging, rewarding, dedicated, self-motivating, courageous, life changing event, and committed journey you'll ever experience. By far most the biggest investment you'll ever make.

Introduction

Most people never really plan when they are going to have a baby, they just know when they become pregnant, that that time has become the right time, because the baby is coming or going somewhere, ready or not. When this time approaches just remember that you have many options to choose from. Some options will make people happy, while other options will make people protest. Just know that it is your choice and only you and your support team will have to live with the results. Babies will also require a lot more love than they can give, and you will need to remember this when you're feeling stressed and overwhelmed. It takes a lot to care about someone besides yourself, especially if you are a teenager with or without a support system; or if you've never had the opportunity to experience the great feeling of someone caring for you, or you caring for someone else. Selfless service will be endless.

Now first things first, there is no such thing as a perfect parent, but there is such a thing as a loving parent.

Love hard and love unconditional. Remember this: a parent is one that sticks around especially when one wants to run. Therefore understand, "You are your baby's first everything." Make sure that all the decisions you make from this moment on are made for the better good of the child (within reason). The child comes first at all times (unless they are young adults and smelling themselves). Besides, the sooner you realize that you are no longer in charge, the easier raising them will become. Teach them to be independent because you will spend enough years having them depend on you. Mark my words, if you haven't before, live each day to the fullest and mark each memory with your child as though it is your last. Be grateful that you are alive and healthy, and regardless of the circumstances in which you have found yourself, make the best of it. It is what it is. Understand that at times everything in life is going to seem like it is going downhill. Use this time to find your strength within the eyes of your child, the strength from your parents, and the faith that your God has given you, and pull yourself together. Remember, in order for you to provide for your child, you must first provide for yourself mentally, physically, and emotionally. So make sure that you find some me time. Me time will allow you to have patience and be most appreciative when you return to your child(ren). They will need you now more than ever, and you will need them as well. Life is full of surprises and journeys, and thanks to you, you are contributing to the biggest journey of all, "Life." The world will be forever grateful for your contribution and I would like to be the first to say, "Thank you."

Rather you are single, married, divorced, widowed, same sex marriage, foster, or an adoptive parent, you are on your way to becoming a parent today. Being a parent is a 24 hour a day 7 days a week job. You do not get to select the time and day you want to become a parent. This is not something you can fill out an application for and wait for a follow up phone call. This is it. You cannot quit, you cannot call in for a day off, nor can you get a refund or ask the doctor for an exchange. This is a lifetime investment, so invest carefully and understand that your investment is going to go out into the world for a test drive; therefore, be mindful as to what you are putting out into society for others to come in contact with. For the most part, your child will be a representation of who you are or who you were while raising them. You cannot learn parenthood, you have to live it. You can only learn to find a balance to get you through the challenges; therefore, pick your battles and learn when to throw in the towel. Know that everything about a child is a miracle and you should treat their lives as such. You must choose to lead, guide, and mentor throughout their lifetime. You're new at being a parent, and they're new at being a person. Their storyline will be your lifeline. Yet, it is your responsibility to teach them to strive hard and acknowledge their skills to help them bring out the best version of themselves; so they could be proud of who they have become and hopefully who their God wanted them to be. In the end, learn from your mistakes, and prepare them to handle their mistakes diligently while making the best of every moment. Teach them that there will be consequences for their actions or actions alike. You only have today, the now, this second. There are no do overs, and each child will have a different journey. Now while that's marinating, let's step into being pregnant.

Nothing should ever be stronger than a parents bond. Know this and embellish it. Soon you will be a parent f-o-r-e-v-e-r.

Being Pregnant

Here is a quick talk tip: The second that you find out that you're pregnant, before you can tell anyone, immediately go home, pull out your suitcase, and stick your life in it. Pack your most favorite outfits, shoes, and accessories. Take all of your money out of the bank, buy a bottle of the most expensive wine you can afford, and drive to the highest elevation in your town and yell, "HELL NO WE WON'T GO" and toss that luggage over. Why, because it is the last time for a long time that you will be number one, have control over what happens next, can be selfish, stingy, inconsiderate, arrogant, sexy without being conservative, free and spontaneous, and fancy. Now don't get me wrong life has not ended just yet, but believe me when I tell you, it has JUST begun. Get ready for the ride of a lifetime. Instead, you can load another suitcase up with a budget, a plan, some organizational skills, a giving attitude, sharing, caring, consideration for others, turtlenecks, flip flops, loafers, sweat suits, tennis shoes, a new caravan, and friends with children. Why, because it is the only thing that is going to save you at this point besides the support of your faith and your family. Notice how I continue to repeat "faith and family" the two most important elements that holds a family together, and makes raising children lighter.

Depending on when you conceived this child, this is when the doctor will tell you how many weeks you are and inform you of how far you are within your first or second trimester. Please call the doctor back and inform him not to flatter you by misinforming you. It is not called a trimester but a life master because it is going to be that long before you can get that child out from underneath your wing and on their way; even then some will return. At this point, you are going to have to master parenting through your experiences and the experiences of others in order to be as successful as humanly possible. *NOTE:* Successful as humanly possible is not measured by the amount of trials and tribulations you have or will endure, but by how you've chosen to deal with it, and what you've learned through those difficult times resulting in grounded happiness.

Some days you'll wake up and feel as though you're on top of the world, while other days you'll feel as though you're beneath the surface. For some reason, no one within 100 miles is pregnant but you. Why is that? Why does it look like everyone is looking at you? Try to use this time to make everyone around you feel as though without you the world would end, because it is you that have chosen to help keep it populated. NOT THEM.

For those of you that have it, there is no such thing as

morning sickness it is daily sickness, personality change as in Bi Polar Queen, and is the only time you will get to eat destructively without criticism while acting crazy without reason. The criticism will come two years later when you're still wearing that baby fat. Thank you, Kimora Lee Simmons. This will also be right around the time that you'll need to ante up and go shopping for maternity clothes. Why it is wise to take your best friend if you must ask yourself? It isn't, you see your best friend reminds of what once was. They think the clothes are so cute and little while you're looking at the prices and adding up the numbers in your head to decide what you can and cannot afford. Things are settling in. Reality has just introduced himself. *Hello!* Honey you need your parent, a guardian, or a parent figure because now is the time for strength, wisdom, and a common denominator. Be open to everything and everybody. Here is also where you will realize a lot of what your parents have said and done in reference to finances making sense; therefore, doing what you need to do not what you want to do may come in handy sooner than later. Similac or Gucci, pampers or Coach, the light bill or the bar, or working or calling off. My favorite line to my children is always save, save, save, and to make sure that you're making good choices when you're deciding the difference between a need and a want when you are spending. That advice went in one ear and literally ran out the other. Children will have begging down to an art, from the time they are born until eternity. As they get older, you will begin to see that their hands are forming like cuffs. You will work hard to give them things you didn't have growing up, and to ensure that your struggles are not as tribule as your parent's struggle; and they will work hard to demand more. As you give them the world, they will demand the universe. Watch what I tell you. Mm, hmm and remember their money is accepted in the same stores as your money as they get older.

Labor and Delivery

This is **THE** one time in your life that no one will ever be able to prepare you for. For some mothers, and for health reasons, labor and delivery can happen in two ways: (1) through having a C-section (this is when the doctor will cut you across the abdominal area, take a good chunk of your insides out, and help welcome your child into the world); or (2) what some of us believe to be the pleasures of natural birth (this is when you look and act like the incredible hulk by trying to push a whole person through your safekeeping without an epidural). Epidural is defined as a lifesaver. Don't go into labor without one. It works miracles. Take it from me, I got the T-shirt. It's cheaper and easier in the long run. While some may find natural birth easy, it is just as excruciating as a C-section. The only difference is: one you will participate in, and left with long term side effects (urinating on yourself every time you sneeze, cough, laugh, jump, fall, or get frightened; and lifelong stretch marks while being on a never-ending diet, and left walking like a cowboy in turned over boots). The other option will leave you feeling like you're about to experience a combustion through the abdominal area (bloated without gas and carrying weights around your stomach). This is solely up to you, your health, and the doctor knowing what he is doing. Check his credentials and don't forget the biggest side effect of them all, THE KID! Girl bye.

Although, you cannot wait to see the creation that has developed from the likes of love and passion, (described as blood, sweat, and tears) the life of the little one gets closer and closer. This is one of the many obstacles you will have to endure to get there. Just exhale. On this day, you will get a pass to squeeze, scream, and shout ridiculously at everyone in sight to include your parents (MOM). Take advantage of this moment because it is rare. You'll feel better later. You really will. Everyone there supporting you will think this behavior is normal, and for the most part it is. But if it isn't, you just run with it anyway because there might not be a next time. Just as no one can prepare you for this, you wouldn't want them to steal the thunder of this once in a lifetime moment anyway. Instead, you'd want to give it all you've got, and invite everyone to the birth that you owe a good licking to. Take advantage of this opportunity and let it all out. In fact, while they're rubbing you and bringing you ice.... grin and bear it. Plan your punch. Now brace yourself because after this endeavor, it's all about getting your body back, preparing for your new life, and introducing the new you and him or her into the world.

No one I've known gave birth and looked into their little one's eyes and said, "Hey little one, I plan to mess you all up and cause you all kinds of pain and suffering." So, realize this, and decide to be the best parent you can be by making choices that best suit the child, not yourself. Therefore, you are not putting human wolves out into society to eat up the rest of the vulnerable community.

CHAPTER 1

After Birth

Finally, when you leave the hospital do not forget to ask the doctor for your diploma. You have just graduated from the University of Life, with a double major in Parenting and Life Skills, and a minor in Scams. You should receive your JD in law, PhD in nursing, psychology, teaching, tutoring, life coaching, human resources, criminal justice, accounting, project manager, education, coaching, chef, janitor, stylist, relationship coordinator, scams, con artist, liar (yes liar), fashion designer, promoter, public relations, security guard, DCFS Coordinator, safety and don't forget your five Mens Rea coupons for the few times you will snap on your child or for the sake of your child. **NOTE:** *Be mindful of the name you choose for your child. The name should represent who your child could or should be. Let it stand* for something genuine. Not like Mercedes because your child cannot be a car or Claritha because you couldn't decide which friend to name her after. STOP!

Once the baby is born of course, everyone is going to want to hold him as well as tell you what to do and how to do it. Let them, it is the only time you will have a lot of visitors, a lot of attention, and a break that you will long for later. People that will visit today will be scarce tomorrow. People that will also come to your baby shower are really celebrating the last time they will see you as who you once were, because now you are someone different, "A Parent." Babysitters are literally a dime a dozen. Either they are nowhere to be found or they will not pass your home mothering security check (HMSC). *"Make sure that you trust your babysitter because you will think about the baby all night long to where you will not be able to enjoy yourself. It is also within your best interest to involve yourself around those that have a child or children, so you can feel most comfortable about your life changes."* This is also when you will feel like a super mom, well you're not. You're new. So, get over yourself and allow others to help you in areas where you'll need it. Especially, your mother figure. Listen and learn and don't be judging your birth mom (whoever loved you enough to raise you) or comparing yourself to her because it is her morals and beliefs that are going to be the foundation of your balance, good or bad. Many times, I hear words come from my mouth and almost choke because I can literally hear my mother's voice. Her actual voice. Talk about scary. There will be many times that you will do things JUST like your mother that you've said you'll never do. Get over that too. On this day you are finding out that you are in many ways just like her, and now you'll understand some of her choices more clearly. One of the best things my mother has ever said to me was, "As my personal life changes, my outside life must change as well." (Edith Haire) This means when you have a child have friends that have a child, when you have children be friends with those that have children, and when you are married have friends that are married or couples. This will make choices easy for you as a partner, parent, or spouse. Birds of a feather will at this time flock together. This is true in every sense of this metaphoric statement. The key element here is to ensure that just as your outward appearance change (child (ren), marriage) that your mindset (thought process) must change as well. You will become more immune to birthday parties and trips to the zoo, than concerts and adult gatherings that do not involve children.

Post Pardon Depression

Some women will get it, while others will not. This is a very dangerous and sensitive area; therefore, get help as early as you can, and be open to all the assistance that is available to you. Remember to do what is in the best interest of the child at all times.

Stillborn, Crib Death, Miscarriage, and Abortion

This very seldom occurs, but does happen. Let me be the first to say, "I'm sorry for your lost." As hard as this may be, if there are other children involved, they still need your presence and love. Mourn, but try not to allow it to take over who you are, especially if others still depend upon you. If this was your first child, remember that God knows what's best; and it's ok to try again when you're ready and able, if you choose to do so. Also, there are no correct words to say unless one has experienced this before. Meanwhile, I'll be praying for everyone that has and for all safe deliveries and choices for all.

Breast Feeding

The most courageous woman on earth, is one whom uses a breast pump, because she believes that extracting her breast with a pump that looks like a science project will extract her abdominal area back to the six pack that only she once knew she had. NOT! Go ahead ladies, and after sucking your veins through your breast tell me how that six pack is looking now.

Breastfeeding is something very special for a mother and her newborn child. It is a way of bonding and communicating nonverbally with your child. Many people believe that breastfeeding feeds the brain. If that is true, then all mothers should breastfeed their children until they graduate from high school. Okay maybe that was a bit extreme, but it would be a guaranteed return on your investment. Smile, smile. Breastfeeding is also some-thing all men will want to try at some point in their life. Please ladies, do not believe that when they see you or another woman breastfeeding that they view it as nature, because they don't. They are wishing that they were a baby again, just not imagining their mother on the other end. Not a good look fellas. Not a good look. I'm shak-ing my head right now because this is one of the many silly things they will want to experience, and you should let them. In fact, tell them if they swallow (I'm smiling) that it will make them closer to the child. *Psst. There is no relationship between breastfeeding your partner and bonding with the baby, but it is our little secret and worth every bit of trying. Hey and if your child have a full set of teeth or walk up to you at 5 while you're playing cards with your friends, pulling on your shirt, and says he's thirsty, he want some milk? I'm telling you right now, I'm the caller. I'm calling DCFS because that ain't right. That ain't right!* Also, mothers the longer you save that umbilical cord, the longer that child will live with you. Just kidding. No, I'm not. Ok, Yes, I am. *Whisper* No I'm not. Hold on, I'm asking my son if he looked for a job today because he is still on his way at 30. Take it from me, hold a waiting to exhale party and burn all that baby stuff you think is so cute because at 30 it isn't; and don't forget to drop that umbilical cord in the fire to honey.

CHAPTER 2

Turning One

When babies are born they slowly develop the strength of a super hero and the brains of Albert Einstein. While you think their first real words will be gaa gaa goo goo, it is translated into "I am in control from this point on. Not you mommy and definitely, not you daddy." Remember I said this.

Sometimes when a child is within his or her first year they are so good that you tend to think, wow we can do this again if they are all like this; or I think we need to contact the hospital because I think they gave us the wrong baby. This is easy. We got this baby. Yeah, well newsflash, everybody gets an easy baby. Wait until that second, third, and fourth one kick in, all of that extra happiness is going right down the incinerator. All of it. Some babies will make you want to become the

President of a baby committee, while others will make you want to shove them back inside. Just understand that if you are blessed with a child that is busy crying and not sleeping, giving him back is not an option. Chances are you have the new Mariah Carey or the next president in your arms (just dream so you can get through this stage); therefore, you just have to find a way to connect and move forward. Whatever technique you used to stop your child from crying, remember it as you go through the different stages in raising him or her. Also, remember that the same technique will not work on every child, nor will it work every time on the same child. Make yourself a screaming song and tell your child to scream, scream, scream, because unless something is seriously wrong, they will not stop until they get what they want (the beginning of the real journey). You should also make sure that there isn't anything seriously wrong before removing yourself from the equation and allowing them time to calm down. *Do not create any crazy habits with your child that you will expect others to uphold when they're babysitting.* Therefore, you will need to be more creative, and innovative. This will allow you to find new and more inventive ways to reconnect in the future. Keeping them grounded and staying connected is a priority, because as times change so will their behaviors. Boy 'am I pulling my hair out now. My daughter is 14 and smarter than me, because "she knows." In fact, my daughter just informed me that she needs to live her life. Meaning, I should allow her to do whatever it is her friends are allowed to do. Now if you know me, you would know that Alaska will have 12 months of darkness before that happens. She also states that when she's a parent, she is going to allow her children to do whatever it is they want to do. I just looked at her; I'm like "girl whatever and we'll see how that turns out." In fact, don't call grandma for bond money because she won't have any. Honey Bye.

Now for a morale booster: Get your smallest shirt from the closet and put it on because your breast should be engorged, and make you feel like a brick house (play the song, get a drink, and reminisce). Just don't forget your pads. You wouldn't want to look like you just left a wet t-shirt contest, besides once that milk dries up and your breast hardens that brick house assumption will go right out the window, record scratched, party over.

Teething and whining

A baby teething is like a mother giving birth. Okay not exactly, but they both are screaming from the acnes and pain that they are experiencing from something big coming from something small; yet something that would leave them with a smile forever. Get ready to have your patience tested on levels you never knew existed. The crying, and all the sleepless nights will be your real test of growth and patience. You will literally have tooth-picks, or tape on your eyelids to help keep them open. *If you've ever been kissed by a person and it felt like they have slobbered all over your face, this is what it feels like when your child is gnawing on your jaw when they're teething. I don't know where that came from; I just need-ed to say that. No relevance, just funny and true. At least I think so.* As for the screaming, sometime your child will be screaming so loud and for so long, that if you are driving, you are going to want to pull over and put the whole car seat out. YOU CANNOT DO THAT. That's against the law, it just feels good saying it. Instead, become the singer that we both know you're not by cracking the window (make sure the sun is not shining in on the child), playing some soft music, and letting her rip. If you are at home, lay down with the baby resting his or her head on your chest, and start rocking and humming. *BEWARE,* this will be the best damn sleep you will ever get in your life. In fact, you might wake up and find that the baby has been up for a bit. Do not be alarmed, just be aware and don't let it happen again. Don't feel like you're a bad parent either because you over slept, just look around to see if everything is still intact and if anyone else is or was there; then get up like nothing happened. We all have done this at one time or another. Actually, we (Mr. French) have not. During this year while your child will be teething which mean a lot of crying, wanting atten-tion which mean a lot of crying, being hungry which means a lot of crying, needing to be changed which means a lot of crying, learning to walk which mean a lot of accidents and crying, being sick which means a lot of crying, or just growing pains, and in this case you should be crying. Don't feel pressured just adjust. These are stepping stones in their lives, but notches on your belt. Remember this will be one of those times you'll need to remember what techniques you used to get them to stop. Buy teething rings, or teething gel, talk and read to the child, and improve your rocking skills. It works wonders, and remember they are learning you. You must stay in control. Pay attention to how you choose to handle this. Example: giving the child a teething ring, doing a little rocking, then putting them down is way different from giving them nothing, and just picking them up and baby talking them to death in hopes that they will stop. We've all witnessed this before, when you lean towards the ground to put them down, and they climb back up while gripping your neck like alligators are on the ground swarming around your feet, and your neck is their safety branch. You do not want to get to a point to where you cannot put the child down; otherwise, they'll cry forever until the both of you are sick. *This is one of those habits babysitters and grandparents cannot break and may not want to deal with.*

It is a gift to say, "I Love You" as often as possible and a Sin not to. Discipline them with a soft voice, and praise them with a louder voice. There will be times that this will be a challenge for you, if it is, just assess yourself and try that conversation or technique again later.

Remember it is not about being a perfect parent, but a loving parent. This is a learning experience for you as well as for the baby. When raising a child, the roles are constantly changing from teacher to student for both the parent and the child. My motto has always been "You get one chance to be a decent mom or dad, so you might as well try to be the best parent you can be." There are no redo's; otherwise, we would all be in Utopia (the perfect place) doing it or at the hospital exchange unit (there is no such place). You will make mistakes along the way, just be there for the fixing. Also, remember from the ages of birth to 5 that their brains are like sponges so fill them up with good lessons and memories not learned lessons and consequences. Although, they may not be able to communicate verbally all the time, they are able to communicate and comprehend from their points of view some of the time. Make these times happy times to remember. Remember your God is watching you, and the rest of us are praying for you.

Dirty smelly diapers/pampers

Remember that all babies stink. Please do not think that your child lay golden eggs because gold caviar smells as well. This is the perfect time to get back at the father. In fact, tell him that this is another father's test. Tell the father that you read somewhere that changing diapers/ pampers would determine how close he will be to the child (but it's our secret). Inform him that it also means that if your child is a boy, he is more likely to follow in his footsteps (ladies make sure those steps are some good footsteps, because we know. Okay? We know). Good luck on that one. Just remember all diapers/pampers get thrown out immediately into the outside garbage. Great remedy to keep the animals and rodents out of your garbage can.

Walking

Nothing is more fascinating than watching your child trying to achieve the goal of independence. One of those goals will be learning to walk. Learning to walk will be one of the two most important days of your life. (1) Your child learns to walk while in your life, and (2) someday that same child learns to walk out of your life and into the world. Nonetheless, both important times will bring you tears of joy in a way that will have you crying like a newborn baby.

Someone somewhere said that babies learning to walk provided a certain level of freedom for the parents, or that it places you in a different category. Um, don't be like me and forget to ask if that category was a good one or not. What I did learn was "This is WAR." Put your game face on, grab snacks, toys, a baby leash if you believe in them, and get your tennis shoes because baby got wheels. Today they are learning how to walk, and you think that it is cute, and tomorrow they are running to the mountain top like there really is a promise land.

Now ask yourself, who is this really supposed to benefit? They do not want you to carry them, instead they want to walk with pride in front of the other babies in their strollers and prance around like they have been doing this for years. Do not give them that freedom in public places unless you are prepared. They WILL use you to see if you've really earned that notch of patience on your belt. Listen and repeat after me, "I did not earn that notch of patience on my belt; I just passed to the next level. The baby really is in control." Now you're ready. Load that stroller up as a reminder to the baby that this is where they will be if they break out with any of that funny stuff. Kids really can act up in public. You know why, because they are testing you. The toy store and the grocery store doesn't look anything like the living room or their crib. I'm just saying. Nevertheless, walking means accidents, and accidents means crying. Encourage their walking by picking them up when they are not crying as a reward for just being them, but be there for them if they fall to let them see that you've noticed them. **WARNING:** Do not pick your child up because they are crying and want their way; otherwise, you'll never be able to put them down. *Again, do not start habits you cannot break, or expect others to practice.* It's bad for business. On another note, remember to child proof the home like it is Fort Knox. They run fast, then faster. They crawl in tight places, play in the garbage, climb under the sink, and slide down the stairs. They laugh, they cry, and they scream just like little characters. You soon begin to wonder who this child is, and what happened to that cute little baby I just gave birth to months ago. They're GONE. Loooong gone.

CHAPTER 3

Turning Two

*A*lways *be prepared for opposite day. This is the day that your child will do the opposite of everything you tell them not to do. This day will come and go throughout the life of your child. Remember I told you so.*

Most people call this age the terrible twos because this is the age that your child will begin to explore everything there is to explore (the home, store, and anywhere you take them). They will put everything they see in their mouths, they will touch everything they see, they will slob on everything they touch, they will scream when they want things and scream when you give them things they don't want. They will crawl on the floor and find things you dropped when you first moved in, and they will hide things and squeeze in places you can't reach them. They will prefer to wear that dirty nasty smelly diaper/pamper, and they will rip that dirty nasty smelly diaper/pamper off when they are tired of wearing it in places that you would prefer they don't. They will kick and scream when you're getting them dressed, and be filthy by the time you're dressed. On your most tired days they will not sleep, and sleep when you want them to take pictures. Do not put your most favorite outfit on them until two seconds prior to the moment if you want a successful moment; otherwise, I told you so. Children at this age are so cute, cuddly, funny, daring, and fearless. They can also be a hot mess, clingy, mean, afraid, and challenging. By the end of this stage you would have learned to have more patience, be humble, fearless, organized, disciplined, and manage your time. Understand this, their terrible twos are really opposite year because everything you will want to do they will not, and everything you don't want to do they will. Therefore, everything that could go wrong will, and everything you want to schedule and organize will not. They will do the opposite of almost everything you say while smiling and laughing as they do it. They will challenge you to learn what their limitations and boundaries are instead of you teaching them theirs. Don't fold, especially if it is something you may regret later. Otherwise, enjoy the little creative blessings. Grin and bear it because you still have your threes to worry about. So, as we soldier's say, "Ruc Up" because you're in for a new adventure.

CHAPTER 4

Turning Three

Congratulations, your child has a new name called "Toddler." They are so cocky and demanding at this point because they know you better than you know them. They spent their twos studying you and your behavior while you were supposed to be teaching them how to behave. They are confident in their walking, mumbling, and exploring. They know how to hide themselves and things. They know what they can get away with and what they cannot. They know who they can get away with it with and who they cannot. Your toddler feels dominant. Watch out. Mean what you say and say what you mean. This is how you will stay in control. If they learn nothing else at three, make sure they learn that you mean business. Just as you will develop a look of seriousness, they will develop a look of shame, mischievous, sorrow, and toughness. The best part about this age is when you talk to them they can begin to respond with clear and direct answers (they have been talking since they were infants, you just couldn't understand their language. Well, now you can). Oh, yeah and they mock everything they see and hear by choice so be mindful with what you say, how you say it, who you say it to, and what you do around them. They also know what belongs to everyone in the house and they know what don't. What's funny today will be embarrassing and a visit with the principal tomorrow.

Biting and hitting

Biting and hitting will become your child's defense mechanism. For every time they feel pushed into a corner, or do not get what they want, watch out because either teeth or an object is coming your way. Children continue to bite other children because you the parent has not been firm enough to stop them. For instance, teach them that biting is for eating. In no way should you allow the child to think that they will get away with biting anyone; otherwise, that'll be a hard habit to break that no one will want to deal with. This habit will also keep you on guard because at some point someone is going to want to bite them back, and you know this. As for hitting, perhaps you as a parent should give second thoughts as to how, when, or if you're hitting them when you're mad. Also, limit the viewing of the Power rangers, Spiderman, and Ninja turtles as they are no longer just characters on television, because you have them live jumping, flying, and hitting throughout the house. How do you stop this behavior? There is no right way, but good examples will go a long way. On a different note, buy some pajamas, make a cape, and jump and fly around with them so you can distinguish that as play time and not as revenge time or acting out time. This way you can control the situation, and stop them when you don't want them jumping and flying around the house like super heroes or destructively hitting others as a form of resolution. Be mindful that different solutions work for different children at different times for different reasons and different situations. Just nip it in the bud prior to them entering pre-school, because this will not go well with the administration and definitely not the other parents. You'll be looking like you're raising a wolf, and I just can't see that going over too well. *Psst.....Please do not hit, kick, or pinch someone else's child when nobody is looking. You are too big to be trying to get your child's lick back. News flash, it will not resolve the issue. All the child is thinking about at this point is that you hurt them, and what a giant wolf you are.*

Potty

It's potty time. Time to train the little one on how and where they must go to use the potty. Naturally, they will christen the house with their dirty nasty smelly little diapers/pampers by taking them off any and everywhere

19

they see fit. They will run, and stick their hands in it, and touch things. You will be disgusted and outright livid. Be prepared. There is nothing in the world like the smell and the smile on their little faces when they are about to rip that dirty nasty smelly diaper/pamper off. *NOTE: For the most part, do not EVER leave a child unattended on the changing table. THIS IS UNSAFE.* They will hide or sometimes stand firmly in the corner while nature is taking its' course. Potty training is a must for preschool and it is your opportunity to get that money back into the budget; therefore, consider this as another duel between you and the child. Stay strong and try to show them who is boss. Also, there are no limits to what you would try in order to get them on that potty, and there are no limits to what they will do to not get on it. A potty song is also a good idea with a little dance as long as the dance and or song ends in the bathroom and on the potty. Remember they are fast and creative so you must be on your toes at all times. Once this is conquered you and the toddler will feel a certain sense of independence and power. Your pockets are lighter and so are theirs, if you know what I mean. Just remember, the duel isn't over just yet.

Body slide

Now that you have survived their terrible twos, and creative threes by receiving a few notches on your belt, you feel like you have one up on your child. Well wake up, didn't I say you needed to be on your toes at all times? The body slide has just entered into the duel and it is something you just cannot get away from. When your child is upset and do not want to be touched or picked up, he or she will perform the body slide routine on you. You must brace yourself, be strong, and be prepared for a new version of reflects that you didn't know you had. Plant your feet about 30 inches apart, bend your knees a little, and prepare to grip and clutch. This is when they will lift their arms in the air as far as they can reach, and pray for grease to be released from their underarms, while they twist their bodies, and drop their legs as if they are paraplegic. You must be fast to catch them, or they will fall. Their bodies will somehow become very slippery and feel boneless. You will forget that they are crying because you will be trying to understand this new thing that they're doing with their body, and why. This is dead weight that will somehow be heavier on this day than ever before. Nothing will stop them from playing dead body man but giving them their way or leaving them alone until they can pull it together themselves. You try playing the dead man body game at the same time and watch the glare in their eyes. They think its real funny when they see you acting like them. Mirror, mirror on the wall who's in control of it all?

Blankie, bottle, and binky

Is the binky not enough? Well, well, now as far as the blankie, bottle, and binky are concerned, if these items are not already gone; then it's time to par and I don't mean golf fellas. Any child that is still carrying a blankie (blanket), drinking from a bottle, and sucking on a binky (pacifier) at three, should be in the Guinness book. Just like any child ridding in a stroller at six and can stop it with their own feet, should be sent to babynile (juvenile) detention. I'm just saying, these are the items that you used to calm them when they were restless babies or teething; now you have to get them back. War again I tell you? It never ends. Choose your battles because if you think potty training was a challenge, you are in for a different kind of ride. Giving up the bottle might be easier, so I would suggest that you start there. The blankie and the binky won't be. The bottle can be an easy transition if your family eats at the table as a family, because the little one will be glad to have the same dishware (big boy sippy cup) as everyone else at the table. So, gift wrap that sippy cup, buy a balloon, and prepare to celebrate. Celebrating a massive change as such is always a good way to transition the child from one stage to the next. They love celebrations and praise. They also love feeling like they are transitioning into the big people's club. **NOTE:** *Use funds from your savings account, IRA, TSP, or 401K to purchase the best sippy cup money could buy; because when the liquid is all out, across the room that cup will go. That is translated to, "I want more **NOW!**" Baby practicing reflect techniques.* As for the blanket and the binky you are on your own because there is something inside of them that tells them when you are coming for those items. If you try sliding the blanket from their little hands in their sleep, they will tighten up their little grip. If you wash it, they will know because it is all out of slob, similac, sleep, snot, and their personal smell. If you pull on the binky, they will suck it back in or give a little whine. This will be inevitable. Also, when they are awake please don't make a trade with snacks because the little ones will bribe you for the snack, eat the snack up, and then scream at the top of their lungs until you literally throw the binky in their mouths from across the room. *This is another one of those habits others will not want to tolerate.* Don't put hot sauce on it either because that's just mean and hot of course (that worked in the 60s, 70s, and 80s....that's child abuse today and I think it was child abuse back then, nobody just told or cared). Find ways to keep them occupied, so their minds are off the blankie and the binky and on the task. And STOP calling it that. It's a blanket and a pacifier. Ugh, sometimes we cripple them before we know it. And Santa Claus is real, so is the Easter Bunny, and the Tooth Fairy. Yes, I did just capitalize these characters like they're nouns. Stop! They are, and stay away from your friends that do not indulge in these times, because they (or their kids) will ruin it for you and yours.

Hey, let's not forget the little one that keeps walking around the house all day, just saying "Ma" "Ma" "Ma" because he or she likes the sound of it, right Tyler? Boy oh boy, talk about patience. There aren't enough notches you could hold on your belt to help get you through this stage; therefore, let us pray. Lord help me? Start singing "I Need You Now," by Smokie Norful.

CHAPTER 5

Turning Four

B e on the lookout for bullying because it can start as early as 4 years old (preschool). Do not allow your child to get away with doing things to others at this age because it is cute, funny, or for the sake of "they're just kids," and do not allow it to happen to your child. You are your child and students protector. This could be the beginning of something horrifying for them or someone else's child. Either way, pay attention to your child and re-member to display good behavior. Also, be mindful and try to make good choices with your chosen consequenc-es for their actions. Know destruction when you see it because you will see it again within 18 years. Try to deal with it head on before it becomes something worst later, like a habit. Remember that your toddler will display his or her anger the same way you have expressed yours in their presence, or with what you have allowed them to get away with. Environment is the key (home and community). Use this time to talk, cuddle, and develop a good strong bond with your child. Remember you are the parent, not the child, or their buddy. They have to know who is boss early on, and the boss is not them.

Preschool

This is a sad time because now the little person that you have spent so much time molding to be thoughtful, to share, to be polite, and to pick up after themselves; will now mix with others that may have been raised by wolves. Peer pressure starts early on we just like to think that it starts when puberty kicks in as a teenager. Instead, it starts now. The pressures begin with the teachers and their peers. Your child will begin to pick up behaviors, choices, and expected results from those behaviors of other little children and their adult mentors. They will say things they heard other children say, and do things they see other children and their school house mentors do. They will learn and watch the reaction of their teachers as well as their peers, and try to get away with it at home. Let your antennas up. Inform your child early on; what happens at school (Vegas) stays at school (Vegas) it does not come home. It is a must that they learn early on that the teacher's rules are the rules appointed by the school board, and mommy rules are appointed by the home board; yet enforced by the Superintendent named,

Spanky, timeout, no T.V., no outside, and no play dates. Therefore, mom supersedes everyone. Including dad when he's not looking. He didn't hear that did he? Okay, moving right along.

CHAPTER 6

Turning Five

From this age on your child will be invited to many parties. Understand that the gift must match the party. If the parents went out of their way to have a lavishing party, you must buy a lavishing gift. If the parents baked a cake and put some M & M's and chips in a bowl, you buy a card and match the dollars with the age of the child. It sounds mean, but some parents have parties just to get gifts, gift cards, and money. We're on to you.

KINDERGARTEN

There is no day like today. Today is the first day of the rest of your life. Another notch on the belt named *Free at last! Free at last! Thank God Almighty, free at last (American Phetoric, 2001)!* There is nothing more important than going to Kindergarten, buying that cute little back pack, and all those school supplies you know your child isn't going to use. Dressing them up in that little outfit that nobody think is fabulous but you, cutting and curling their hair, and walking them down the street for drop off with pride. Looking into those little eyes, and holding up the line to give them all kinds of advice as if they're going to remember it. You thought you were so ready for this day, yet you are crying harder than the child. The teachers are pulling the child away, not knowing that it is you that is gripping the child. Well, wipe those tears moms and go find yourself something to get into. Do not go home and anticipate the time your child is coming home. Do not go into their room and reminisce through their things, and do not sit in the carpool line waiting for kindergarten to let out. Aww, what the heck it's the first day why not, but tomorrow you need to get yourself some business because you are free at last again, at least until they are released from school. Remember not to have too much fun, because you might forget to pick the little one up. Then YOU'LL be in the principal's office whining.

Today they will come home from school so proud, and so vibrant talking your ears off with more informational documents than the law allows. You must listen, you must be interested, and more importantly you must fill out all those documents the school sent home and return them as soon as possible so your child isn't looking like they're being raised in the woods with their papers being blown all over the place. Two rules: Your child does not want to be last for pick up, nor do they want to return to school without all their documents signed. Please keep this in mind. Day two is the biggest day of them all. Your child will bring home their first art picture that you will not be able to describe or recognize, but must pretend that you know exactly what it is, and it is the most beautiful picture you have ever laid your eyes on. You learn humility, and you learn how to compassionately lie when you have children. This little masterpiece goes right up on the refrigerator, and the 8000 baby pictures come down.

Riding the bus

If your child is a school bus rider, do not drive behind the school bus to make sure that the driver goes straight to school. I am sure the bus driver knows his route. If your child is afraid and you feel you need to follow for the first couple of days to make sure that your child is okay, or that he or she does not get off at the wrong stop; then by all means go ahead (yeah right). Other than that, stay clear. Do not stand outside the bus waving and crying like Niagara Falls, and do not go home and reminisce at all the good and difficult times you've shared until this day. Just go home, and if anything, remember what it felt like to be free for a moment before Dennis or Matilda was born. Do not pull out any old photos, blankets, bottles, or binkies. Instead, talk on the phone without interruptions, get the laundry done for once, prepare dinner, pay some bills, and fix yourself up before everyone gets home. Just enjoy the moment that will continue to end sooner than later. In the end, do not be that crazy person that zooms pass the bus to beat the driver to your home, because you were sitting at the school (because you never left), in your pajamas, without your nails, toes, and hair done. Scarf sideways, smoking a cigarette waiting for your child to be dismissed. Now you need to road rage it home looking straight crazy. Girl bye. Ok I did that x3. Looking a hot mess.

CHAPTER 7

Turning Six

I hope you are prepared for this, because this is the age that every other word in your child's mouth will be, why? Why, because the child is curious, and of course the fact that it is going to hit your nerves in a way that you will never understand the level of patience God has given you. Why, because they are supposed to be, and this is how they learn. They just do not know how to be quiet or stop. Why, because they do not want to stop, and they are trying to fill their little brains with as much information as they can. Why, because they want to know how much information they can fill in their little brains. Why, because that is how they think and there is a possibility that they think they will be able to see this information, or someday know more than you. Why, so they can begin talking back by telling you what to do, or acting as though they were here before you. Why, because they do not know what is going to happen to them when they began that journey. Why, because they are not as smart as they think they are. Why, because it was not meant for them to raise you; otherwise, you would be asking them why. Then, you would be working their nerves, and they would be reading this instead of you. Why, are you kidding me just be ready because you are in for the journey of a lifetime. On your best days and definitely on your worst days, your child will be smiling and asking you why to each and everything you tell them. Be patience, be educating, be ready, and be well. As my mother use to tell my brother, "Boy, go rest my nerves." You're going to need this phrase and you can have it. Why, because my mother has used it up and soon your child will act like they know it all thanks to you. Why, because you answered all of their questions instead of telling them to go rest your nerves. Why, because you didn't instead, you thought they were too big for naps. Why, because you just found out that they are not. **NOTE:** *Remember naps are applicable until you stop them.* Why? Really, because they just are? I'm screaming. lol

CHAPTER 8

Turning Seven

This year your child is really going to be looking crazy. Karma returns when you least expect it. This is
when your child's teeth will begin falling out one by one
and they will not keep their mouths closed for nothing.
This is a personal gift to you. They will take all of their
school pictures proudly, as they should, but with a little
extra just for you. They will have mastered the perfect
smile you have been trying to teach them for the past
four years that they never got right, just because you
wanted them to, *until today*. They will want you to order
enough pictures for the world to view, (hint) but your
budget and pride will not allow you to do so, especially
for those pictures that have smiles with only one tooth
dangling on each side of their mouth, or the one big
tooth in the middle in front of their mouth. This is when

they are at their proudest for some reason. This is not the picture for the refrigerator, but they will want it on the refrigerator, and the wall in the entry way. *These pictures and more are reserved for later usage like prior to leaving out for the prom. This is reassurance of no funny stuff, unless you want kids that look like this.* Now, new house rule, all entry way photos are for babies and graduation. Hey, whatever works as long as you understand they are going to show that picture off every chance they get. You just have to be aware of when and where they do it. Parents, you must always be one step ahead of the game; otherwise, you're slipping and their actions will definitely show you when that happens. Your kid must learn early on that you will find out EV-VER-RY-THING-GAH they get into prior to them getting into it. Keep them on their toes as well.

CHAPTER 9

Turning Eight

There are two types of children you can have at this point. One that bounces off the walls or one that jumps off the walls and ends up bouncing. Either way, you'll have yourself a bouncing bean, over active, super playful, energetic child that will be in and on everything you call furniture. Everything you say to this child will be sent in one ear and out of the other like a train running through a tunnel. They will want to try everything there is to try that equals dare devil. More time will be spent in the ER or at the doctor's office, than at home. This child will be on first name basis with the personnel running the doctor's office, because it will be their second home. This is where your doctoral skills will need to come in handy. In fact, in most cases the child will know how to patch up some of his own wounds; therefore, the doctor's office will only be needed for surgery type injuries. The little one will at this point have fallen from a tree, fallen off his bike, fallen off the bike ramp, broke his arm, broke his leg, twisted his ankle, caught lice, caught the measles, caught the mumps, caught the chicken pops, caught poison ivy, scraped an elbow, needed stitches, needed a cast, and just stressed you out beyond control. You will find out that the child has allergies and need glasses, or have cavities and need braces. You name it, they will have it, get it, and get it again. They will want to be everywhere, doing everything with anybody who is doing anything. Everyone can start calling you Doc because you will feel like one. Instead, use this time to go on Sharebuilders (online brokerage used to purchase and trade stock) and invest in medical and dental stock, because your child will make you rich and poor at the same time. You might want to take the time to climb to the top of your highest elevation again to scream once more, because this will be one of those trying stages where you may want to cash in on one of your Mens Rea coupons. This little busy body will teach you a whole new level of patience and furry. Independence is their new way of defining themselves. Just let them go and be wild. Better to get all that savage out of them when they're young, then when they're teenagers, because later on the stakes are much higher. Much higher! In fact, rent a cabin, drop them off in the woods, and let them be literally raised by wolves. What the heck jungle boy did it. Teach them to live off the promise land. Okaay, I was just kidding. Don't do that. That's another thing that's against the law. You have to be out there in the woods with them and the wolves. I'm smiling. Every now and again I get lost in the moment and forget I'm not talking to myself. Don't do that! Joke. Why am I still smiling? Also, don't force fancy pants (cute girly stuff) on your daughters because they will want to wear everything but girly stuff just because you want them to. Ughhh. Hey, you can get them back when they're teenagers by buying matching outfits and sitting at the table with them and their friends acting 16 again. See how they like that?

CHAPTER 10

Turning Nine

Turning nine is the age that your little big child will begin to try to analyze everything that they know at this point. If you send them to the store, they will think it is ok to spend a few extra coins in hopes that you will not notice the coins missing. They will also try to spend all the money on the one item you sent them to the store for; therefore, they will not have to go to back any time soon. They will want to walk home alone or ride their bikes to and from school to be a part of the pack rat biker's crew. Screen their friends and their friend's parents. Do understand that their friends at this point are important to them, which is all the more reason for you to put them through the friend selection process. It sounds crazy, but unless you want to be driven out of your mind, you better become the president of the friends' selection committee.

Your biggest challenge will be your child wanting you to be just like their friend's parents, "The Werewolves." Just like there is peer pressure, there is adult pressure. Now is the time like never before to join alliance with your spouse or partner, because your child's fake psychology techniques will begin to kick in. This means whatever their friends parents allow, they think you are supposed to allow, NOT! Maintain your home values and morals. Remember the forces, the strength, and especially the love is supposed to be stronger within the home, than outside the home. Let them know you were in the honor society at the Wolf Academy. Every place their friends can go without supervision, you're not supposed to allow them to go without supervision (their friend's parents are not cooler than you just because they allow more space, make sure you point out the I told you so's). Remind them that their friend's parents are possibly mean and that the only real reason they allow them so much freedom is so they can be free again. Then say, "You don't want to be free anymore that's why you had them." Then smile, hurry up and turn around, and leave. This way they will not get a chance to analyze your face. Now parents although this is sounding like a really good idea as I read it back to myself; keep in mind that these little darlings will possibly have to care for you later on in life. They get no face reading time during this stage. None. Choose your battles and your words carefully. This is still a challenge for me at 50. I still rush to my room and crack up in my pillow.

Nine years old, is the beginning age of sleepover heaven. Do not view sleepovers as a break, or a day off because it is not. Your child could return home with lice, ringworms, mono, and many other nasty diseases that people have and do not warn you about, because who's going to say it? "Of course, your child can sleep over, oh, and mine have lice." Keep them home already, many kids are raised by wolves anyway. No reason for you to drop off a child, and pick up a blood sucking wolf. You better take a look around and make sure all the subjects in those photo albums don't have four legs with their tongs hanging out. Hmm. All children need to go to sleep and wake up in their own beds, because who knows what traffic is running through someone else's house these days. What looks good on the outside is way different on the inside, always. Nine-year old's are older two-year old's. They want what they want and will manipulate you to get it. Nine is also half the age of becoming a young adult. They will not think that they are adults, but they will want the freedom of one. They know everything, and you will not understand anything because you were never nine. As if you were born big and dropped down on earth like Mork, but as their care-takers. Take a deep breath again, and choose your battles because this is only the beginning, and it just might be the only battle you get to choose from and win.

Telephone

I'm not quite sure if you are aware of the telephone phase. Ok you are because you've done it before to your parents. The only difference is, you knew the results (The look of death. This look meant everything a parent knew was illegal to say and do, but was meant and read between the lines). This is when the house is very quiet and your child is doing what kids do, while allowing you peace of mind. They are so good at this time, until the phone rings. *RIIINNNGGG! RIIINNNGGG.* When this happens, they somehow appear through the surface of the walls, carpets, and doors. It is like magic and no matter how many times you tell them, while talking through your teeth, "If your sibling isn't on fire or bleeding to death do not interrupt me." They will still continue to resurface. You know why, because they know you. They know you've been waiting for this phone call all day, and so have they. Now it's a matter of how much they can get away with, and which part of that conversation to dive in on. You want privacy, and they want a BIG FAT YES to whatever it is they have been waiting so patiently to ask you. Remember I told you, THEY ARE SMART. Prepare yourself, they will disappear when you hang-up the phone like Houdini, and reappear like ghost when the phone rings again, and you know what? You're not even mad, because they know just when to get out of the way; therefore, thinking about how they interrupted you is the last thing on your mind. Children have a magnetic mechanism that is connected to the electricity in the telephone system. So, when the phone rings it sends a signal to all children that draw them to the main phone line in the house. That main phone line my friend, is the line that is in your hand. Hello? *Remember I said, "They have been studying you since day one while you were supposed to be teaching them." They weren't star-ring at you when they were infants thinking, "This is my mommy." Ha. They were reading your mind while trying to figure out how many years it would take before they would be in control. Watch out!*

Sleep

This moment is more excruciating because kids know when their parents are asleep that the only word that utters from their mouth is YES. Yes, is the first word that utters from your mouth because you are having the dream of a lifetime. In this dream, you're kissing Denzel Washington, having dinner with Matthew McConaughey after cruising around town in that Cadillac MLK, or watching them mud wrestle for your love while you're sipping on some nice chilled wine. I have one even better, a nature walk in the woods with Clint East Woods. So, they come into your bedroom and stand at the foot of the bed and ask for the keys to your car, your credit card, all the cash in your purse and pockets, and if their punishment can be lifted and they spend the weekend with their boy/girlfriend in Mexico on you? Your only response is yes, yes, yes, go, go, go. In the meantime, their thirsty little selves are rambling faster and faster through your things thinking you are rushing them to clean you out, when the two of you are not even in the same space. You don't even have children in this dream. You know why this happens, because they studied you. They know your strength and more so your weakness. You need to step your game up, take the spark plugs out the car, put pennies in your pocket, and change your credit card limit to $10 a day. If this doesn't help, bolt the bedroom door, set the house alarm, and change the alarm combination that only you know. Anything after this, back to the woods they go, you been got, and we're pulling your gangster card.

CHAPTER 11

Turning Ten

Normally, at this age if your child were born before September 1st they are in the fifth grade. This is right around the time they believe their lives are changing. They are top dog at the elementary level. They are more concerned about fitting in than anything you could imagine. Friends that they grew up with are no longer of interest to them, because of the fear of getting ready to transition into middle school has taken priority. Those that are out spoken will ask questions or give you signs loud and clear; while those that are not will become more distant. Those children you need to pay closer attention to. Keep them involved in sports, activities, and or things that interest them. This is your opportunity to bond again or create a bond tighter than what you've had before. What you do not want is for your child to feel like they need to do anything possible to fit in with the wolves, or that they have no one to turn to. They must be happy within their own skin. Parents, make them proud of who they are, show them where their journey began, and guide them towards a path of righteousness. You as a parent must ensure that the foundation you built within the home based on love and strength is stronger than any foundation based outside can offer. Family quality and quantity time is even more important at this time. The more time you spend together as a family, the less time they'll have with coming in contact with the wolves or just being introduced into a different world. Peer pressure can become an issue if there isn't any home pressure. Solidarity of the home can be possible with or without two solid parents, but co-parenting is a must if possible. It is the messages and the love that child receives, how they receive it, and how they deal with what they receive, that's important. Remember for the better good of the child.

Your child will also go through several hormonal changes and not all the changes will be physical. Some of the changes will be mental. If they have not already began to want to think for themselves now is definitely when it begins. Your child is going to want to know why he or she cannot do, be, wear, or say the things their friends can do, be, wear, or say. Don't say anything, just give them the look. One eyebrow up, and one eyebrow down. You will be the mean parent and your partner will be the nice parent. You have to remind your child that you are not in a parenting contest and that their best interest is the only reward for you. You must pick your battles with your child in accordance with the impact the battle will have on your child, their studies, as well as their personality changes, and the home environment. Everyone has a role. Play it. Teach it.

If you have a daughter she will be concerned about when her breast will grow and when her menstrual cycle is coming so she can catch up with the rest of her buddies. For some reason this is when they think they are grown. News flash: they are not and please do not treat them like they are. Children are not grown until they are living on their own, paying their own bills, and swinging by to drop you off some cash, just because. Until then, continue reading and following this book. Now, if anything, this is when your daughters should get the beginning of the cookies story (Cookies story is defined as part I of staying away from boys' period). Tell them not to worry because as soon as they receive their menstrual cycle, the sooner they will be praying for it to go away. Besides, someday later in life their new buddy will appear "menopause," and that's when they should be begging for their menstrual cycle to appear. Begging. Daughters are also great manipulators. They will for some reason think that you are supermom and that you should carpool their friends and feed them (order fast food) just because they asked in front of them.

Tell your child kindly that the next time they try to put you on front street in front of their friends; that you will explain to them in front of their friends about how poor you all are, and if you could spare the gas money to feed them, you would. Remember moms, you are the first and the best version of a woman for your daughters to learn from. Teach them well, and let them know that you have game.

Your son on the other hand is concerned about when he will get to touch a pair of breast and not get caught. **TIME FOR PART I OF THE TWO PART TALK FOR HIM** *(Boy don't get yourself in some trouble you can't get out of)*. He must get these crummy little thoughts out of his head. Be prepared though because he won't. It is all a part of life. Instead, use this time to teach him about respect for a woman because he was born from one. Dad's and father figures, the way you raise him to view women will be the way that he will grow to treat and respect women. If the home is without a father figure, find a brother, uncle, in-law, nephew, or boys club to teach him things he cannot learn from a woman. Then fine tooth those lessons and prepare him as best you can. Puberty has nothing to do with this stage except the fact that boys will no longer think that all girls have cooties. Puberty begins very early for some and late for others; nevertheless, it comes, and you must get prepared for it, if you haven't already.

Let us not forget to talk about the shower, boys will

go into the shower and hide behind the showerhead to ensure that the water does not touch them. They do not like water at this stage unless it is at the pool. They reek like raw fish, feet, sweaty tennis shoes, butt, and garbage. On top of it all, they will smother it with deodorant, clean clothes, and not a dash but a full bottle of cologne that creates the worst smell ever. You can tell them a thousand times to take a shower, but it will never happen until a little girl embarrasses them by telling them that they stink. Nothing else will work because I have tried. N-O-T-H-I-N-Gah. Stinky boy is a legendary stage that you cannot avoid. If there is testosterone in the house, stinky boy will also be there.

CHAPTER 12

Turning Eleven

Middle school is a very nervous place to enter for most children. They feel stressed because it is now that they realize once again that all the children are bigger and older than them. It is again the first day of school. Be mindful of the new friends and their family members your child will become in contact with. You never know the traffic others have floating through their homes, and you do not need your child picking up on habits you cannot literally give back. Middle school children are no longer cute little baby face children that were in Kindergarten. This is where your child will learn that kids can be cruel. A once was best friend might tell all of your secrets just to fit in, or hold on to them in hopes that you do not leave them behind as you make new friends. Some of these children have already encountered tribulations in their lives that only God could resolve in due time. Your relationship with your child is just as important as the relationship you allow your child to have with their new friends. Make sure that these new friends and their families believe in some or most of the same traditions, moral ethics, beliefs and values as you do. You must make time to meet or acquaint yourselves with the parents of the child(ren) that you will allow your child to spend time with. If you do not, you may regret it later. You do not want to allow little insects (bad ideas) to enter the vents (mind of your child) of your home in places where it may be impossible for you to terminate. Stay in control. Respect your child, their ideas, and their thoughts within reason. Understand you can instill a lot in them, and they still may not turn out like you or the way that you want them to. That's because they are not you and it is about their journey not yours. You are parenting them, to guide them, while instilling certain values and attributes in them in hopes that they use these tools to survive and become the best version of themselves later. Especially, when they are backed into a corner called "challenged or peer pressure." They must have the tools to escape. Listen to what they have to say, and know that they do not think like a parent, they only think they do when they want to be grown. Times have changed, and the way children think, and things are done, has changed also.

At times, your child will disappoint you just as many

times as they will make you proud, if not more. Just remember to grin and bear it because even though that child represents you, they represent themselves more or at least who they want to be. Recognize early. If there is one lesson you need to remember while raising your child, is this, it is the parents against the world. Every individual your child come into contact with from the day they were born until the day they leave this fine polluted earth, will leave some form of an impact on their life. It is your duty as a parent to intercept and decide what that impact will be, by making a conscious decision of who they come in contact with (when they're living with you of course), and the choices you choose to make. Now a parent cannot control what actions will affect a child, nor how it will affect a child. What they can do is give that child the necessary tools to be able to create a way to lessen the blow (devastation) and move forward.

CHAPTER 13

Turning Twelve

If she looks at me like that one more time and deep breathe or he slams and locks his door again, (it is not against the law to take the door off the hinges) it is on. Your child is at the age where they have a mind of their own and want to use it and lose it. They have learned about their constitutional rights as citizens of the United States and think your home is City Hall. News flash, protest elsewhere. That was school, which is also what school was supposed to teach them, they just forgot to teach them the next chapter called "Mommy Amendments as citizens of 123 Get in that X%!* Doc.." As parents you have a right to amend, append, modify, revise, or revoke those rights if they do not snap out of that learned behavior and bad disposition. Now unless he or she wants to be convicted and do some real hard time; they might want to take this court supervision (grounded) and take a chill pill.

Parents you can get all the goods from your children at this age because this is also the age that they fight over everything especially the front seat of the car. Sit back and get your popcorn because at this moment there will be no more secrets in the house. Let the telling begin. You will find out who broke what, who did what, when, where, and how. You must referee at this time. The juicier the news determines who gets in the front seat. There is a difference between tattle telling and snitching. Tattle telling gets you rewards from your parents and snitches get you stitches. **NOTE:** Do not, I repeat, do not give this child too many rewards because they will be telling on their siblings as a career. Keep switching the kids back and forth until you have confirmed everything that you already knew, or until you have had enough. Then, act as though you are upset at the information you have just learned, and to seal the deal, put them both in the back seat. BAMM! Now you can tell their father or your partner to pay up because you won the bet. The bet was that you already knew what was going on, they just confirmed it. Why is it hard for the father figure to understand that the mommy figure knows everything? We truly are seven years ahead of the game. Um? I guess they are from Mars and we are from everywhere else. Oh, well.

CHAPTER 14

Turning Thirteen

This is the most amazing time of all. Your child should be experiencing the privileges of being top dog also known as an eighth grader at his or her Middle School. Parents prepare yourselves because this is graduation year, and your child will feel like they have earned a right to do everything their graduating class will indulge in, and they have. This is a time to jump for joy because just as it seems you are halfway there, honey a new show is about to start. **NOTE:** *If they did well, go out of your way as much as you can to give them the grand slam graduation party. If they barely made it, perhaps they can go to somebody else's grand slam graduation party.* Do not run up on the stage, sprinting pass your child, and snatching the diploma from the principal. Although, you did the work, put in the labor, and suffered through

55

the process, it is their diploma. Restraint parents restraint. Remember your relationship is very important at this stage. Regardless of the trials and tribulations you may have encountered, what you may have learned from it, and how you may have chosen to deal with it; it will now show in your relationship and communication with your child. Just remember you need them just as much as they need you. Let them know how important their role is to you and the household. Give them some responsibility and hold them accountable for their actions. Praise them loud and immensely when they do well, and discuss what the effects will have on everyone for their actions peacefully when they make choices that have consequences. ***NOTE:*** The hardest part in raising a child will be having them to have continued faith and belief in you as a parent and as their safe haven; while continuing to value your opinion with full trust in you and the result.

By this time many things would have occurred or is about to occur, between now and the end of summer. Puberty is really in the air for most teenagers. Most young ladies are going to want to start wearing make-up; while most boys are going to be concerned with everything from pimples to wanting to date. ***PLEASE NOTE:*** it is not okay for your child to get belly rings, tattoos, or date at this age. It does not make you a cool parent by allowing your child to come and go as they please nor speak to you or others like they are adults at this age. Please keep them grounded; otherwise, they're going to be a work of art for the rest of the community to have to deal with. Choose your battles carefully, and know that every choice you make without their best interest at heart will justify the means of a consequence. Teach them to pay attention to small details instead of being carefree, and to know that there is a place for everyone in this world. Whether it is on earth, or beneath the surface. If you have made it thus far, you are doing something right and there are only four more years before letting that kite go. The only advice I can give you once you've reached this point, is PRAY. Hard! In fact, beg.

CHAPTER 15

Turning Fourteen

Oh, my goodness, and to think you thought you were in a good place. Some children will already be in high school, while the late bloomer December babies will be just entering. Fresh meat is the term used for the incoming freshmen. This child is a full fledge teenager. Your child is feeling like a mailman being chased by a Rottweiler with a bloody steak in his or her back pocket. Game on. Once again your child is the newbie, and will do EVERYTHING there is to do at this point to fit in, to include, challenge you. GIRRRL. Don't start. All I can say at this point is Damn, Damn, Damn for what you are about to encounter. *NOTE:* Each child is loved differently in accordance with their needs and therefore, should be treated in accordance with that level of love. I just came up with that, just to remind you to continue to love them because I'm afraid for you at this point, but there is some truth in those words.

There are three types of children to have at this point 1) the overachiever, 2) the underachiever, and 3) the coaster. The overachiever strives to make you happy, and you are happy. They are your example of a model child. In fact, they would be the very reason you would choose to have more children. They are responsible, accountable, giving, polite, ambitious, strong minded, creative, athletic, trustworthy, and helpful. This child was possibly conceived when you were happy and in love and made good decisions. Understand that this child may be so focused on making you happy that he or she might have forgotten about themselves in the process. Embrace this child, do not allow him or her to feel like they must live up to your unreachable expectations, but the expectations they create for themselves. Ensure that they are reminded that you are blessed to have them as your child, and that you want them to be happy. Meaning, you are happy only if they are happy. Allow them to follow their dreams not yours, and remember the stress of living up to you is way deeper than that of their peers. Love this child for who he or she is and who they want to be.

The underachiever on the other hand, is the one that blames everyone for his or her own indiscretions'. They either have problems making friends and fitting in, or do not know which direction to go in. This child doesn't want to join any sports activities, clubs, or teams. This child is barely passing all their classes, irresponsible, rude, a taker, mean, low self-esteem, talk back, sometimes disrespectful, and nondependable. The look did not work on this child. This child is driving you up a wall. This child is not happy with change, but happy possibly with me time. Find out what is eating at this child and try the parenting thing all over again. Burn all the black stuff. I'm just saying. Although, you only get one chance to be a decent parent, it does not mean that your job is ever done. At different stages in your child's life you get to revamp the relationship sort a speak. Instead, it means you have one lifetime to get it right. Be patient, be understanding, and more importantly listen to the verbal and especially nonverbal communicational signals. Listen, it is not that this child is displaying underachieving values, this child is just confused. It's like being chemically imbalanced. Something in this child's life got scrambled and needs to be unscrambled so they can get back on track. You must find out what makes him or her light up and watch them glow. You may need to spend more time with this child than expected in order to get him or her back on track, I promise you it'll be worth it in the end.

Finally, the coaster, this is the child that cruises through life. This child has average grades, does what he or she is supposed to do on most occasions, stay out of trouble but is a bit mischievous at times, sometimes play sports and sometimes not (more athletic than everyone put together), has a huge sense of humor, most times a momma's boy/girl, and believes in living each day to the fullest, while literally having NO worries. None.

When does it end? N-E-V-E-R.

Every child deserves to be loved equally from their parents, but differently in accordance with their personalities and needs. When you have a child, you must commit to taking the vow to love, honor, respect, and be there for that child until death do you part as you would your marriage or any other commitment you take seriously or to heart. Embrace your child because it takes a lifetime of embracing, forgiving, and building to be at a place of comfort with decent results.

Parents don't be a fake and don't be a fraud. We know what we are putting out there in society. No one knows our child better than we do. Lead by example and take responsibility for your parenting skills.

Sometimes you may want your child to be more than what they want to be for themselves, or even think they are capable of being. You as a parent must remember that this is their journey; therefore, accepting them for who they choose to be is worth more than anything else you could ever give them. You can only wish the best for them, and accept the best from them, whatever that is.

Education

There are two things I want to leave you with now that your child is in high school. Planning and preparation for the Graduation to Transformation. Do not allow your student, the next generation of our great nation, to just enter high school and show up. Showing up is easy. It is just showing up, passing your classes, and finally graduating. Well, anyone can do that. It is part of your duty as a parent to ensure that they are in the right classes that will prepare them for the journey that is to take place afterwards. We are all mamagers. Start asking them if you haven't already what it is they want to be when they grow up. Look up the schools they are interested in or that carry the major they want to study, and find out the requirements to get into that school; then plan and prepare. Get them the training they need, provide them the skills to achieve, and teach them to adapt and overcome and push forward. More importantly, get them to attend. Attend meaning, being a part of what the school has to offer, explore, excel, and then graduate with a future to look forward to (transformation).

There are only 5 things a person could do in this life: (1) go to college, (2) get a job, (3) grind for your dream, (4) join the military, (5) or become a menace to society which isn't an option so we're down to (4). So, let's get started, many schools take 21-23 credits to graduate. Well, the school will make sure that your student has that. What you need to do as a parent is to make sure that those 21-23 credits are conducive to what their plan is after graduation. No one ever sits and discuss the planning for that transformation. Do not allow your student to enter on their first day without a plan. Do allow your student to research where it is he or she wants to attend afterwards (college isn't for everyone, but they must go somewhere (military, job)), and prepare themselves academically and mentally for that change. Explain to your student over and over of the four positions a person can take in this world: college, military, job, grinding for their dream. Challenge your student and keep them hungry for their choice. Help your student to plan and prepare for their next journey in life; otherwise, there will be no next journey. Explain to your child that school is not just about embracing the fundamentals and the fun. It is about transforming into a lifetime of success with the skills and training to guide them through the process. Remind them that you do not and will not finance failure, and that failure will never be an option. Keep them around positive and outgoing people, and remember this is not an easy task because of sports, popular kids, and peer pressure. Just come up with ways to keep their eye on the prize by involving them in activities (college visits, camps, and summer classes and seminars) that remind them of their goals.

Educate to graduate, to transformate, or make a mistake.

Finally, everyone can go to college, but everyone cannot attend college. Going to college is showing up for four years, changing your major over and over, not indulging in what college has to offer due to too much partying, and graduating with an average to low GPA, but with the expectation of landing a job. *NOT!* Attending college means to be involved. It means to explore who you want to be, take trips, volunteer within the community, do internships, network, join clubs, teams, and groups. It means to modify laws and make laws. More importantly, it means to stand for something, be something, create something, take advantage, and graduate with a competitive GPA that lands you the job of your dreams. Don't just go, attend because bigger stakes are involved, and don't allow anyone to make your child feel that their educational choice is not a good choice, or the best choice for them. It is not where one starts, but where one ends, and what they do with the time spent in between.

TEACH THEM, REACH THEM, and continue to PREACH TO THEM the desire to HAVE MORE, WANT MORE, AND LEARN MORE.

Now before I get to deep, let me say this "After you've had several children to complete your choice size of a family and one of the children just can't get with the program? It's not your fault. That child is just chemically imbalanced due to something in the gene pool on their daddy's side." I'm smiling because it is my story, and this is how I wish to tell it. Shhh here he come, hurry hide the book. Truthfully, this child just needs more of you because something along the way (happened/changed) got in his or her way and they got lost. They were not able to grasp the tools you gave them to figure things out. Help them find themselves.

The Letter

Dear Parents and partners,

If you are looking for a quick fix on how to raise a child(ren), then stop looking, there is no quick fix. Raising a child will be the most challenging obstacle you will ever endeavor. You will say things and do things that you will be sorry for later; just make sure you acknowledge those things sooner than later, and be accountable for them as you embark on this journey. Don't be stubborn because you will teach them or one of them to be just as stubborn as you.

Whether you as a couple chose to take on this journey as a couple or as an individual; there is no amount of money that could make up for the special moments or trials and tribulations that an active parent goes through daily while trying to raise a child(ren). If you start off as a team you must end up on that same team, "TEAM CHILD." Therefore, when you are called upon for your assistance, your advice, or your love, be available and be present. Let no man or woman keep you from being a parent, because no one will love your child more than you. Nor will there be any love like the unconditional love you will receive from your child. Regardless of the good, bad, or ugly you bring to their lives, they will always and forever remain faithful, committed, caring, and loving to you. All children want from their parents is love, and discipline. Do not allow them to seek this kind of unconditional love from strangers, street thugs, friends, mates, or some mean family members; because no one will ever measure up. Love thy child unconditionally, and remember that they are your rock because you are theirs. Besides, as long as they know and feel that you love them, they will always prevail, prosper, survive, and excel.

Sometime as a parent, you might have to cut yourself into many different slices at many different times in your life in order to make this parenting thing work, or to be somewhat successful at it. Be active, be responsible, and be accountable for your position as a parent. Don't pawn this job off. It is not a bargain. Besides if you made it thus far, there's a possibility that you've done a good job. Throughout all the challenges that raising a child will bring, to include puberty, your menopause, and man's midlife crisis; don't consider yourself lucky to have survived it all, instead consider yourself blessed to have been able to be a part of it all. **NOTE THIS:** THE hardest time you will have raising your child, will be "A

Lifetime." No stage will be easier than the next, so try to prepare as your family grow. Each stage will feel worse than the next, just focus on conquering it instead of challenging it. More importantly, as a dear friend passed on to me (I'm not mentioning his name because he's not smarter than me), they are not you, so do not expect them to make the same choices you would make (In my head the whole time I'm thinking, "Why not?"). Instead, guide them to make the best possible choices for themselves and the situation they're in; then remember to love them for who they are. Okay he didn't say all that. I'm making him sound to intelligent. Hmm. Now when you make it here...you can say, "You've been parenting, because you been doing the damn thang." Wouldn't it be nice though if you could just buy a bag of love, a certain type, and just give it out, and that works? Just brainstorming.

Baby Bylaws

YOU ARE your baby's first everything.

Remember if you stay calm so will the baby.

Don't let your baby be free spirited and do what they want, because they can't behave like that with others. Some people prefer limitations and boundaries.

Don't get upset when you cannot find a babysitter. It is your child not theirs. The sooner you come to terms with that the easier it will be for you.

Only involve yourself around people and activities that revolve around children; otherwise, you will feel stressed and overwhelmed.

Stop dressing the baby so he or she can look cute while they sleep in their crib. Who's looking? They smell good no matter what, and most people only want to pick them up to smell them anyway. It has nothing to do with the outfit, believe me, nothingah.

If your child does not rest when you need him or her to, take a moment and lay down with them so they get a feel of that resting heartbeat of yours, then tend to your business later in peace.

If your child is acting out in a store remember EVERYONE in the world was a child once and has done or experienced the same thing. Don't be embarrassed. Next time leave the house with the child's favorite toy, a snack (dry cereal), and a drink of some kind. Depending on the tantrum, this is a time to decide if talking or a little pat on the butt would work. Perhaps it's too late and the child is sleepy because they should be in bed.

You will be invited to many parties. Understand the gift matches the party. If the parents went out their way to have a lavishing party, you buy a lavishing gift. If the parents baked a cake, and put some M & M's and chips in a bowl; then you buy a card and match the dollars with the age of the child.

Understand this, all the cute little clothes you buy your child from the time they are born until they are seven is your fantasy, not theirs. By this time, they are figuring out who they think they are by torturing you with the ugly gothic look or the boy look. Let them be, but when they become teenagers flip the script and see if they like having a gothic, boy look, or old maid of a mom. In fact, buy matching outfits.

Kids are precious. All they want to do is see you, smell you, and study you so don't be absent.

It is easier to take a few minutes and play with your child or answer their questions than to be nagged by the whining to a point of stress.

Teach your child to say excuse me early on and then make them wait, but do turn around and acknowledge them or respond. It teaches them patience.

Say no before the child reaches their terrible twos so they are not saying no to you in their terrible twos. *NOTE:* There is no such thing as terrible twos, babies are terrible from the time they start talking until they move out, if ever.

Get all the kisses you can while your child is asleep, because when they will wake up that party will be over.

Tell them the rotten tooth that the dentist pulled out is nonrefundable to the tooth fairy; and the next tooth only get a refund of 50% due to their negligence (not listening to brush for breakfast and bedtime).

As they get older treat them as they treat you, so they get lifelong lessons hands on.

Take as many pictures as you can when they are snag-a-tooth because they look funny. In fact, call them in the room when you are having a bad day and a drink, and let them be at their funniest, so you can get a good laugh. (That's a get back at them technique). They just look funnier/cute when they are snag a tooth.

When your child does not want to wear his or her coat, hat, and gloves because their friend isn't in the winter. Go buy an ice sculpture of their friend and place it under your child's window; then ask your child if they want to be that to? For punishment give them a smaller and uglier coat to wear.

When the school calls you to pick up your child because he or she is not feeling well, and they come home happy and energetic; take them back to school and tell the school they are cured. If they continue to be sick remember they only get soup, orange juice, and crackers. No TV, games, or phones. This will get them up and running real fast.

Remember children should go to school every day unless the school has a state of an emergency. Snow days do not count. Send them anyway and pretend you did not see the forecast. It's good for them.

Remember when you are punishing your child that you are punishing yourself as well; therefore, be mindful of your punishment. **NOTE:** They will now become creative little con artist. Don't believe anything they say, don't accept any of their display of affection or act of kindness it is all a ploy to get you right where they need you; then they will sock it to you. Prepare to use one of your coupons.

All parents should get five coupons and these coupons should allow you to make it right with your child and God. Do overs are great new chances for both parties. TOO BAD IT DOESN'T WORK THIS WAY. I don't see why it can't, cats have nine lives? Hmm.

For the child that just irks you, irk them back and just understand that it is just where your relationship is.

A child does not have to have everything they see, they must learn restraint. In fact, when they are born spell their name the way it sounds, then tell them not to touch anything in the store unless it has their name on it. Pow!

Do not allow your child in the same room as you and your adult friends. What you all are talking about is not their business. Besides, they'll start the gossip and you'll be trying to figure out what happened.

No matter how mad you are of the absent parent never down play him or her because the child is really only mad at you that they are missing. Besides it is not a good look.

Always accept them for who they are.

ALL children lie. ALL CHILDREN.

Always practice what you preach.

The bigger the child, the bigger the problems. The more children, the more issues.

Everything that you have done to your parents, one of your children will do to you and worst.

Never put anyone before your child. Always listen to them and pay attention to their judgment within reason.

Try to lead by example no matter what the lesson.

Understand we parents do not think we know it all. We just know that we do know more than you (the child), and because a book wasn't delivered when you were born, we made a lot of mistakes that we now know the answers to. You are a product of those mistakes; therefore, relaaaax we fed you didn't we?

Don't ever think they are not sick enough to call a

doctor. If you are unsure always call. Better safe than sorry. Beware they do know how to play sick.

Remember to never compare your children with one another, just be grateful to have them.

If your child gets colic, go in the bathroom, turn the hot water on in the shower and as the bathroom fills up with steam, sit there in the room, on the floor, in a chair, or on a toilet. DO NOT SIT LITERALLY IN THE HOT SHOWER. Allow the steam to clear the child's lungs.

When your child(ren) goes out to play, you must go outside with them and watch them. Your job is never done, especially since the child can walk and talk. They are still vulnerable to strangers.

If you have one of those superman dressing kids with cowboy boots on, or the Alice in wonderland dress up daughter that likes talking to strangers; tell him or her to stop that man is a boogie man. Then enjoy your super hero because they are creative, outgoing, and are expressing themselves.

Oh, oh, oh…. Our children are us. They are everything about us from our strengths, our weaknesses, our choices, and our secrets. They are the present parent and the absent parent. They are those we allow in their presence, and those we take out. Our children take something from everyone we have an encounter with to include those we tell them to stay away from. That's the corner store man, the drunk on the street, the drug addict, the drug seller, the babysitter, the daycare provider,

the teacher, the preacher, the doctor, the lady in the lob-
by, their friends, their parents, your friends, your parents,
the counselor, the coach, cousins, uncles, aunts, and
grandparents. Everybody everyday can have an impact
on your child, so make sure you create a clear path for
them to learn from, because it is too late when they have
picked up on habits they cannot give back so easily.

The hardest thing you will endure as a parent is realizing and accepting that you do not get to choose what
your child will want to become, or when they will want
to start working on becoming it. They have their own
time capsule.

Believe in spanking or not: The first child gets away
with everything because you think it's cute. The second
child gets a warning because of the pass from the first
child so you just think it is a fluke that the third child is
a bit different. This child you spank because it is just crazy that you are running out of excuses and good genes.
Plus, you let the other two get over and you blame the
dad that his family good genes ran out too fast. *This is
also one of those questions you ask your boyfriend when
he asks you to marry him. How soon do your family
good genes run out? Is it after the first, second, or third
child?* Count the Lester's in his family. Dah...Can a child
learn from talk? Yes they can, they can also learn from
a little pat on the butt. This is a choice followed by your
beliefs so don't get out of hand with it. It is to be a lesson
learned not a learned lesson. The Bible says, "Spare the

rod, you spoil the child." The law says share the rod, you spare his life. Mom says, "You spare the rod and spoil the child, society has problems that we all will have to deal with later."

DO NOT USE, MISUSE, OR ABUSE YOUR CHILD IT IS AGAINST THE LAW. LOVE THEM INSTEAD. IT's FREE.

Special needs children

All children have special needs. Some are just born with needs that require special attention. Some needs are internal while others are external. Meaning some needs are mental while others are physical. Love them all and teach them to be loved. Make the necessary adjustments, and enjoy their life and yours, while making memories.

Professionals and care takers:

Understand this, if there isn't a book that comes with the child society says, "Is normal" then there really is a grey area for parents with students with disabilities. With all the classes and professional development training you as a professional must take to understand and prepare for caring for a child with disabilities; it is still trial and error for the parent. The parent gets no classes off the back (after birth). It is just as new to them as it is to you. Therefore, you must always ask yourself, "Do they know?" Be patient, be compassionate, and be understanding. They know less than you. EDUCATE!

Parents:

Appreciate the efforts and advice of your professionals because it is going to take teamwork for the best efforts to be made for your child. Working together is the key. You must incorporate the lessons and information the professionals give you to take home for things to work smoothly at school. Conducive/Cohesion is the key here because the professionals must also understand that the parents have the night life with the students; therefore, they must find a grey area for what will work at home in order to make parenting at home lighter, without diminishing their daily work efforts and vice versa.

Bullying

There is never anything good that comes from bullying. Although, many children will have many excuses as to why they choose to behave the way that they do, you as a parent must be a role model and inform your child that it is unacceptable to make another child miserable. There are no excuses or circumstances that will justify otherwise.

Bullying is never something to be proud of. These are children that are jealous of others due to their own insecurities or children that just wasn't taught that kindness goes a long way. Actions speak louder than words. Children emulate what they see. It is not just foul play when a child says that they are being bullied. The matter requires everyone's undivided attention. Have zero tolerance as a community, parent, or teacher. Be concerned for other children just as you are for your own. Be accountable for the actions you allow and ignore of your children and other people's children. Be responsible.

Puberty

Puberty brings on a different reaction for girls than boys. Girls tend to do what we call "smelling themselves." They are so smart at the mouths or their dispositions are imbalanced. This will be one of those times that you will want to just scream. Things they use to like, they will no longer like. Sometimes they will wake up in the morning on the wrong side of the bed and expect everyone else to cope with it. They are dramatic, selfish, and sometimes just down right crazy. You can chalk this up to their menstrual cycle.

Boys on the other hand are smelly, dirty, and just weird. They think girls have cooties, but they want to touch those cooties; but they need to be focused on touching the soap and allowing the water to touch them. How about that one for touching? Ha, ha.

Self Esteem

Everyone has low self-esteem at one time or another in their life. Yet, high self-esteem is truly about appreciating who one is as a person. It is being comfortable in one's own skin. Self-esteem issues should be addressed very carefully. They are very easy to diminish and very hard to develop. You must spend an enormous amount of time praising your children for their accomplishments and efforts, and correcting their mistakes by showing them examples of choice. Make sure that you are their first fan as a mom and that their dad or father figure is their first hero. If you have a daughter, do not leave room for another male figure outside of her dad to be the first to tell her he loves her, hug her, buy her flowers, purchase her first diamond, treat her like a lady, make her feel special, appreciate her, demand the best of her, and show her that she is loved. If you have a son, do not allow the streets to raise him. Teach him to respect himself, others, and especially the women he come in contact with because he was born from one. Give him his first job, speak to him about life, and fine tune his lessons that could only be taught from a man. Show him who he is inside and out, and who he could be when he makes the effort. The more you appreciate them, praise them, punish them, give them limitations and boundaries, be loyal to them, and respect them; they will appreciate and respect themselves, you, and others.

Respect

Respect any, every, and all people. Teach your child not to concern him or herself with what others are doing, saying, wearing, or the lifestyles they have chosen. Appreciate what you have, and those that made the sacrifice to give it to you.

Teach them to learn to give back to those that are less

fortunate than themselves. Work in shelters, and volunteer in boys and girls clubs. Teach them to understand that there will always be someone that is less fortunate than themselves, so to give back.

More importantly, teach them self-respect. To know who they are and who they want to be, while focusing on being the best version of themselves. No one will ever be able to take that away from them. Loving themselves will be the best defense against all odds as they grow-up.

Humblism

Teach them to stand up for themselves while realizing that some fights are meant to let go and learn from. Absorb the knowledge and synergy. They may never know who they may have to take a step back from to learn from. Humblism will make them more of an adult as many other attributes and lessons.

Pride

Displaced pride can destroy them if not placed properly.

The Pregnant Bible:

When you feel like uncontrollably crying, go around the person that is most sympathetic, so you can milk them for as much attention and stuff as you can get.

When you are feeling fat, go around the person or people that tell you that you're cute no matter what.

When you feel like bingeing go around the people that want to treat you because you are pregnant. Eat healthy. The consequences last longer.

Do not stress over all the things you would want your first child to have, because all a baby need is you and a chest sack.

When your partner is not tentative to your needs, use being pregnant as an excuse to not be tentative to his needs every now and again. This is the one-time ladies we should get a pass to role change.

Wear your partners dress shirts and pants around the house or to bed to show him what a privilege it is for you to carry his child, because this is what he would look like if God wanted man to carry babies.

At their middle school graduation do not inform them that your tears of joy are not because they are graduating, but because you are. Job well done parents. Now for the next stage.

Always remember that children will rat one another out for anything. All you need to do is make friends with the mischievous one, and bribe him or her. They will sing like the fat lady.

There is one thing that all children have in common, I didn't do it, it wasn't me, it's not mine, and I don't know. Remember these words parents because you can use them later when they ask you: Why don't the lights work? It wasn't me. Where did the Christmas tree and all the presents go? I didn't do it. Is the cell phone bill paid? It's not mine. Mom are you cooking today? I don't know. Earn to Learn Kids.

Raising children is like a puzzle, you have to put all the right pieces in all the right places; and when those pieces get misplace, broken, or lost, you have to mend them with a little extra tender loving care, and place them back where they belong. A piece can always be reused (meaning a situation can always be resolved). Resolution and retribution can resolve many obstacles with limitations and boundaries. It is never too late to finish the puzzle.

Nothing will be more exhausting than the energy you will continue to use to replace the skills within your child referencing life planning and preparation; and the less receptive they might become. This is called "Bit by the bug." Save yourself some tears honey and allow them to make their own mistakes. Learned lessons for the hard headed.

Remember that failure is never an option nor is financing failure.

Their life choices will show you when you were on top of your game, and when and where you slipped.

All parents have regrets as well as made mistakes. It is how you've chosen to deal with it, and what you do after the fact that makes all the difference.

Remember when they hurt you'll hurt more, but as they get older remember not to allow their actions to consume your life.

If you're not stressed out or a stressful parent, how else are you planning to get your child on track?

What defines us will be how well we rise after falling.

NO means LOVE. Use it. We as parents have a hard time separating ourselves, because we blame ourselves most of the time for the choices we've made; thinking that it may have caused a reaction for the child, and in some cases it has. Sometime we need to take a step back and assess the situation. Perhaps, it is time to allow that child to grow on their own. As parents, we sometime need a new lesson on crutch, liability, independence, and dependence when it comes to our children. In some cases, we can be the enemy by misrepresenting the identification of the word or feeling of love. Doing more damage than good.

Choose your battles carefully because times have changed, and so have your child's perspective on how things should be; which is way different from yours on life. The supply and demand is different for them as it was for you in your time. Different things have a different meaning and effect on them; therefore, the level of importance is different to them as well

Right, wrong, or indifferent remind your child daily, "I got you."

They can't raise themselves.

Do not give all of yourself to your child, because you have to leave room for you. You will not be their only influence in life, just pay attention to those you allow in their influential space. There will be many times, many places, and many instances that you will not be around. Your influence as a parent (that little voice of yours) still has to be heard in their heads when you're not around. That's when you know you left an impact.

They will compete for your love and attention, and they will do almost anything to get your approval; therefore, do not set the bar so high that they cannot make you proud.

Having a child will make you grow-up faster, pay attention to detail, be wiser, smarter, and love harder.

Parents remember you cannot make all the money in the world. So, when you choose a profession as a career, be mindful of your first career, "Your Child."

At the end of the day, rather you are a teenager or an adult, when you find that you are with child, find yourself a good bible-based church of your choice of religion; then surround yourself with positive influence, and positive support and energy. Understand this more than anything, "Your dreams and aspirations do not have to change or be cancelled, just altered." This is a detour that you would normally have to take at some point for many other reasons, why not for a LIFE?

If you've been blessed with a child, do something with them.

My 25 year old son TJ says, "Too bad you don't get paid to raise children, but you pay to raise them." Who would have ever thought that he could come up with such a profound statement? Um.

Well, since this IS true, pay me because I want my munie. All of it.

My son Tyler says, "As much as I appreciate all the attention, affection, ball games, and parties; a parent should only sacrifice 60% of themselves to their children and sustain the other 40% for themselves. He says, because this thing called "Life" is trial and error for everyone, and that in most cases children will be ungrateful anyway, so why lose you in the process. It is evident that you can't have it all, so why give it all. Just do the best that you can, and stay above the water while in the process." (Whisper, this is the smart one. I wonder if N.A.S.A. could do prototypes. Did anybody hear that?

Nope, nobody heard it. Good). I was on top of my game when I created this child. Start singing the Cupid Shuffle by Cupid. To the left, to the left, to the left, to the leeft. To the right, to the right, to the right, to the riight. Now dip, Now dip. Now you see what I'm talking about. Girrl bye.

My daughter T'ne says, "Ugh, are we still going shopping Mom?" Good genes hit TURBO getting out the way. TURBO!

At the end of the day, children are going to say and do a lot things that's gonna make you want to set yourself on fire. Well, you can't do that either. So you might as well buy yourself a huge bag of sense of humor and grin and bear it.

Do not at any point believe that 100 pages will justify the means of 18 years of raising a child. Each day you'll learn something new about them, and each day they'll change and teach you something new about you. Just remember that people can no longer say, "Babies aren't born with a book," NOW THEY ARE.

BUY ME, you'll need me some day.

STAY PRESENT!

9 781478 753049